The Art of
True Healing

The Art of
True Healing

The Unlimited Power of
Prayer and Visualization

Israel Regardie

*Edited by
Marc Allen*

New World Library
Novato, California

New World Library
14 Pamaron Way
Novato, CA 94949

Cover design: Big Fish
Cover photo: Photonica
Text design: Aaron Kenedi

Library of Congress Cataloging-in-Publication Data

Regardie, Israel.
The art of true healing : the unlimited power of prayer
and visualization / by Israel Regardie : edited by Marc Allen.
        p.   cm.
Hardcover ed. published in 1991 with no subtitle.
ISBN 1-57731-012-8 (pbk. : alk. paper)
1. Mental healing. 2. Meditation.
I. Allen, Mark, 1946-   . II. Title.
RZ401.R37 1997   96-43004
615.8'52—dc20   CIP

First printing, March 1997
Printed in Canada on acid-free paper
Distributed to the trade by Publishers Group West

10 9 8 7 6 5 4 3 2 1

Contents

These are the methods by which the dynamic nature of the subconscious can be stimulated so that the human personality becomes transformed into a powerful magnet attracting to itself whatever it truly desires or is necessary to its welfare. . . .

— *Israel Regardie*

Introduction

So much has been written and discussed lately about healing and the mind. The two are of course intricately connected, and understanding about the mind-body connection has now merged into the common culture. Most people are at least aware of it in some way, through some book or magazine article or TV or radio show. Israel Regardie wrote brilliantly on the subject nearly seventy years ago, and he wrote about the mind-body connection in a way that no one else has written before or since.

I discovered *The Art of True Healing* about twenty years ago, and it has been my constant companion ever since. As soon as I did the Middle Pillar meditation, I had no doubt that every premise in the book, and every promise in the book, is true — and, as you will see, the book deals with not only physical healing, but healing every aspect of our lives. Dr. Regardie says it best:

> *These are the methods by which the dynamic nature of the subconscious can be stimulated so that the human personality becomes transformed into a powerful magnet attracting to itself whatever it truly desires or is necessary to its welfare. . . .*

> *Perhaps sickness is present. Or we need money. Or we have undesirable moral or mental traits — or whatnot. We can elevate our minds by utilizing this energy, so that the desire of our heart automatically realizes itself with practically no effort at all. . . .*

This is a bold premise, and a great promise. In my experience, he delivers on his promise.

The original subtitle describes this book as *A Treatise on the Mechanism of Prayer, and the Operation of the Law of Attraction in Nature.* Though the wording seems a bit bulky by today's standards, the meaning of the words is profound and powerful. Through the exercises in this book, we turn prayer — or any wish for improvement in our lives or the lives of those dear to us — into a powerful instrument for change.

Once you try the Middle Pillar meditation, once you experience its effects, you will probably agree with me that true magic actually exists — and each of us can be a magician, and a healer, capable of improving our lives and the lives of those we love.

Of course, as Dr. Regardie states, these exercises are in no way a substitution for competent medical care or therapy when necessary — but they are a wonderful addition to it, for they are able to aid the healing process in a great many mysterious, profound, and positive ways.

I do the Middle Pillar exercise several times a week, and have modified it somewhat over the years in a way that works for me. (I rarely use sound, for instance.) I encourage everyone to try the exercises, and feel free to modify them in any way you wish. This form of meditation has definitely contributed to my health, success in the world, and ability to help others.

Besides, it's a great excuse to stay in bed in the morning for another fifteen or twenty minutes, and still feel that you're doing yourself and the world a favor.

Marc Allen
Editor

1

The Force of Life

Within every man and woman is a force that directs and controls the entire course of life.

Properly used, it can heal every affliction and ailment we may have.

Within every man and woman is a force that directs and controls the entire course of life. Properly used, it can heal every affliction and ailment we may have.

Every single religion affirms this fact. All forms of mental or spiritual healing promise the same thing. Even psychoanalysis and other forms of therapy employ this healing power: The insight and understanding that effective therapy can bring releases tensions of various kinds, and through this release the healing power latent within and natural to the human system operates more freely.

Each of these systems teaches its own specialized methods of thinking or contemplation or prayer that will, according to the terms of their own philosophies, renew our bodies and even transform our entire environment.

Very few of these systems, however, actually fulfill in a complete way the high promises they have made. There is little understanding of the practical means whereby the forces underlying the universe and permeating every cell of our bodies can be utilized and directed toward the creation of a new heaven and a new earth.

Each one of us has the power to begin the process of reconstruction for ourselves; each one of us can discover the force that can bring us true healing of our bodies and minds.

The central question, then, is how are we to become aware of this force? What is its nature? What is the mechanism whereby we can use it?

A great many different systems have evolved, widely differing processes by which we may discover the presence of such a power. Meditation, prayer, affirmation, invocation, emotional exaltation, and other forms of declaration made at random upon the universe or the Universal Mind are a few of the methods. All have this in common: By turning the fiery, penetrating power of the mind inward upon itself, and exalting our emotional system to a certain pitch, we may become aware of previously unknown currents of force, currents that are almost electric in their interior sensation, and that are healing and integrating in their effect.

It is the willed use of such a force that is capable of bringing health to body and mind. When effectively directed, it acts like a magnet: It attracts to every one of us who employs these methods the things that we require or fervently desire or that are needed for our further evolution.

The fundamental, underlying idea of this powerful healing system is this: In the ambient atmosphere surrounding us and pervading the structure of each one of our body's cells is a force, a field of energy. This force is omnipresent and infinite; it is present in the most infinitesimal object as it is in the most proportion-staggering far reaches of the known and unknown universe. This force is life itself.

Nothing in the vast expanse of space is dead. Everything pulsates with vibrant life; even the subatomic particles of the atom are alive.

The force of life is infinite; we are saturated, permeated through and through with this force, this energy. It constitutes our higher self, it is our link with the entire universe, it is God within us. Every molecule of our physical system is permeated with the dynamic energy of this force; each cell in our body contains it in abundance.

When we consider this force, when we become aware of it, we are then brought face-to-face with the enigmatic problem underlying all disease: If we are filled with this energy, and if this energy is limitless, how can we become depleted of this healing energy, and become unhealthy and sick?

What is fatigue? How can there be depletion of our energy if vitality and cosmic currents of force pour through us constantly, saturating our mind and body with power?

Essentially, it is because we offer so much resistance to its flow through us that we become tired and ill. How do we manage to defy the universe? How are we able to offer resistance and opposition to the very force that underlies our continually evolving universe?

There are many causes of this resistance to the inward flow of the spirit: Most of us were raised to be complacent and confused and even cowardly from childhood on into adulthood, and most of us have a false perception of the nature of life.

The fact that this is generally unconscious doesn't matter — are any of us really aware of all the involuntary processes going on within us? Are any of us conscious of the intricate mechanism of our mental processes, and of the processes by which our food is assimilated and digested, and our blood is circulated, bringing nourishment to every cell?

All these are purely involuntary processes, just as, to a large degree, our resistances to life are purely involuntary. We have surrounded ourselves with crystallized shells of prejudices and ill-conceived versions of reality; we have shielded ourselves with a mental armor so dense it affords no entrance to the light of life that surrounds us and envelops us.

No wonder we become sick, impotent, helpless, poor! No wonder the average individual is so unable to adequately deal with life!

The First Step: Understanding

The first step toward freedom and health is a conscious realization of the vast reservoir of energy in which we live and move and have our being. When we reflect upon this repeatedly, and make repeated mental efforts to make this part and parcel of our outlook upon life, part of the hard, inflexible shell of the mind breaks down and dissolves. Then, inevitably, life and spirit pour abundantly through us. Health spontaneously arises, and a new life begins as our point of view undergoes this radical change.

Moreover, it appears that we create an environment in which we attract just those people who can help in various ways, and the things we have longed for manifest in our lives.

The first step is a purely mental one, involving a change in our perception of life, so that we realize we are in the midst of a vast reservoir of healing energy.

The second step lies in a somewhat different direction: It involves learning a process of regulated breathing — quite a simple process, and, as you will see, quite an effective one when used repeatedly.

The Second Step: Rhythmic Breathing

If life is all about us, all-penetrating and all-pervasive, what is more reasonable than that the very air we breathe from one moment to the next should be highly charged with vitality? To best take advantage of this, we need to take the time period-ically to regulate our breathing in a calm, simple way, and to contemplate that life is the active prin-ciple in the atmosphere.

We should practice this rhythmic breathing at fixed periods of the day, in a relaxed manner, with no strenuous forcing of the mind, no overtaxing of the will. All effort must be gentle and easy; then skill is just as easily obtained.

Sit comfortably, or lie down, flat on your back, in a perfectly relaxed state. If sit-ting, the hands may be folded in the lap, or they may rest comfortably on the thighs, palms upward. If lying down, your hands should rest comfortably at your sides, palms upward.

Let the breath flow in while mentally counting very slowly, one...two...three ...four.... Then exhale, counting the same beat. It is fundamental and important that we should maintain the initial rhythm we have started, whether it be at a four-beat count or a ten-beat count or any other convenient one. For it is the very rhythm itself that is responsible for the easy absorption of vitality from without, and the acceleration of the divine power within.

Unchanging rhythm is manifest everywhere in the universe. It is a living process whose parts move and are governed in accordance with cyclical laws. Look at the sun, the stars, and the planets. All move with incomparable grace, with a steady, inexorable rhythm. It is only humankind that has wandered, in its ignorance and self-complacency, far from the divine cycles of things. We have interfered with the rhythmic process that is inherent in nature. And how sadly we have paid for it!

Through quiet, rhythmic breathing, we can attune ourselves once more to the intelligent power that functions throughout nature. Our periods of rhythmic breathing can be at any time of the day or night when there is little likelihood of disturbance.

We should cultivate above all the art of relaxation:

Learn to address each tensed muscle from toe to head as you sit in a comfortable chair or lie flat on your back in bed. Tell it deliberately to loosen its tension and cease from its unconscious constriction. Think of your blood flowing copiously to each organ in response to your command, carrying life and nourishment everywhere, producing a state of glowing, radiant health.

Begin your rhythmic breathing, then add this preliminary exercise, slowly and without haste. Gradually, as the mind accustoms itself to the idea, the lungs spontaneously will take up the rhythm. In a few minutes it will have become automatic.

The whole process then becomes extremely simple and pleasurable.

It is difficult to overestimate the importance or effectiveness of this simple exercise. As the lungs take up the rhythm, automatically inhaling and exhaling to a measured beat, they communicate it and gradually extend it to all the surrounding cells and tissues. Just as a stone thrown into a pond sends out widely expanding ripples and concentric circles of motion, so does the motion of the lungs. In a few minutes, the whole body is vibrating in unison with their movement. Every cell seems to vibrate sympathetically. And very soon, the whole organism comes to feel as if it were an inexhaustible storage battery of power. The sensation — and it *must* be a sensation — is unmistakable.

Simple as it is, the exercise is not to be taken lightly or underestimated. It is upon the mastery of this very easy technique that the rest of this system stands. Master it first. Do it enough times so that you can completely relax and produce the rhythmic breathing in a few seconds.

2

Awakening Our
Energy Centers

Most prayer and contemplative methods unconsciously employ these inner centers. We would be wiser and far more efficient to deliberately employ this spiritual power and the centers it flows through.

The next principle we must consider is fundamental and highly significant. It is the inability to realize or thoroughly to have grasped its importance that underlies the frequent failure of many different healing systems, whether physical, mental, emotional, or spiritual. Just as there are specialized organs for the performance of specialized functions in our physical body, there are also corresponding centers in our mental, emotional, and spiritual nature.

Just as the teeth, stomach, liver, and intestines are devised and evolved by nature for the assimilation and digestion of food, there are similar centers in the other components of our nature. The mouth receives food, digestion occurs in the stomach and small intestine, and there is an apparatus for rejecting waste products and toxins. In our psychic nature also are focal centers for the absorption of spiritual power from the universe, and other centers for its distribution and circulation.

The dynamic energy and power entering us from without is not uniform or alike in its vibratory rate. It may be of too high a voltage, so to speak, for us to readily endure. Within us, therefore, is a certain psychic apparatus whereby various cosmic currents of energy may be assimilated and digested, their voltage stepped down or adjusted to the human level. The process of becoming aware of the psychic apparatus, and using the energy it generates, is an integral part of this healing system.

Most prayer and contemplative methods unconsciously employ these inner centers. We would be wiser and far more efficient to *deliberately* employ this spiritual power and the centers it flows through.

The Energy Centers

There are five major spiritual energy centers. Since we must name them and identify them in

some way, let me give them the most noncommit-
tal and noncompromising titles imaginable, so that
no system of prejudice may be erected upon them.
For the sake of convenience, we may name the first
one Spirit, and the succeeding ones Air, Fire,
Water, and Earth.

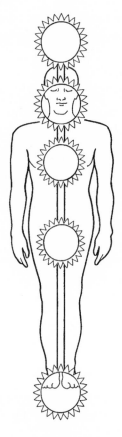

The diagram illustrates the position and location of these centers. It is important to understand that these centers are not physical in nature and position — though there are parallels with our physical organs and glands. These organs exist in a subtler emotional or psychic or spiritual part of our nature. We may even consider them, not as realities themselves, but as symbols of realities — great, redeeming, and saving symbols.

Under certain conditions we may become aware of them in very much the same way that we may become aware of different organs in our physical bodies. We often speak of reason being situated in the head, emotion in the heart, and instinct in the belly; there exists a similar natural correspondence between these centers and various parts of the body.

There are three principal means for us to become aware of these centers, and awaken them from their dormant state so that they may function properly. The means are *thought*, *sound*, and *color*.

First, through our thoughts, we concentrate on

the assumed position of these centers, one by one.

Then we make the sound of certain names, which are to be considered as corresponding vibratory rates to be intoned and vibrated.

Finally, each center is visualized as having a particular color and shape.

The combination of these three things gradually awakens the centers from their dormant states. Over time, they become stimulated, each functioning according to its own nature, and they pour forth into the body and mind a stream of energy and power. Ultimately, when their operation becomes habitual and stabilized, the spiritual power they generate may be directed by will to heal various ailments and diseases both of a physical and a psychological nature. It can also be communicated to another person by a quiet, focused laying on of hands. And by simply thinking, with intent and focus, the energy can also be communicated from mind to mind telepathically, or transmitted through space to another person miles away — for objects in space cause no interruption or obstacle to its passage.

The Middle Pillar Meditation

First of all, the position of the centers as shown in the diagram must be memorized. They are then to be stimulated into activity while either sitting upright or lying down flat on the back in a perfectly relaxed state, just as we did earlier in the preliminary exercise.

If sitting, the hands may be folded in the lap, or they may rest comfortably on the thighs, palms upward. If lying down, your hands should rest comfortably at your sides, palms upward. Calmness of mind should be induced, and several minutes of rhythmic breathing should result in the sensation of a gentle ripple playing over the diaphragm.

Then imagine there is a ball or sphere of brilliant white or golden light above the crown of your head. Do not force the imagination to visualize the sphere of light, for this only results in the development of neuromuscular tension, and defeats our end. Let it be done quietly and easily. If the mind wanders, as indeed it will, wait a moment or two and gently lead it back.

At the same time, vibrate or intone a sound. You have several choices here:

(1) You can simply hum a pitch that seems to resonate, as closely as possible, in the light of your center. Or you can resonate the pitch in your throat center, and direct it mentally to the center of your choice.

(2) You can intone the word from the Judeo-Christian mystical tradition that is appropriate to that particular center. For the first center, the word to vibrate or intone is *Eheieh*, pronounced *Eh-heh-yeh*. (We'll discuss these words in more depth in a moment.)

(3) You can chant an English equivalent of the ancient word. For the first center, the words to chant are *I am*.

(4) You can meditate upon each center,

and discover the words or sounds that have power and meaning for you.

After a few days of practice it will become quite easy to imagine the name vibrating above the head in the so-called Spirit center. This name, this center, is the indwelling and overshadowing divinity in each one of us, the basic spiritual self that we can all draw upon. *Eheieh* means literally *I am*, and this center represents the *I am* consciousness within.

The effect of mentally directing the vibration to the Spirit center is to awaken the center to dynamic activity. Once it begins to vibrate and rotate, light and energy are felt to emanate downward upon and into the body. Enormous charges of spiritual power make their way into the brain, and the entire body feels suffused with vitality and life. Even the fingertips and toes react to the awakening of the coronal (Spirit) sphere by a faint prickling sensation at first being felt.

If you're intoning a word or a name rather than humming a pitch, the word or name should be intoned during the first few weeks of practice in a moderately audible and resonant tone of voice. As skill is acquired, then the vibration may be practiced in silence, the name or words being imagined and mentally placed in the center. If the mind tends to wander, the frequent repetition of the vibration will greatly help concentration.

Let the mind rest in the light of the Spirit center for five minutes or so. Let it glow; feel its dynamic energy. Then imagine that it emits a white or golden shaft downward through the skull and brain, stopping at the throat. Here it expands to form a second ball of light, which includes a large part of the face, up to and including the eyebrows.

We name this sphere the Air center, and a similar technique should be applied to this center as to the previous one. It should be strongly and vividly formulated as a pulsing sphere of brilliant white or golden light, shining and glowing from within.

The name that should be vibrated here is *Jehovah Elohim*, pronounced as *Yeh-hoh-vah*

Eh-loh-heem. Or you can use the words *I see,*
I speak. Or meditate upon that center, and
make up your own words. Or simply hum
into that center's radiant light.

The traditional names for the centers — *Eheieh,*
Jehovah Elohim, and so on — are in reality the
names ascribed in various parts of the Old Testa-
ment to God. The variety and variation of these
names are attributed to different divine functions.
When acting in a certain manner, God is described
by the biblical scribes by one name. When doing
something else, another name is used, one more
appropriate to the actions or states of being that are
represented or described.

This system has its roots in the ancient Hebrew
mystical tradition. Its innovators were obviously
people of exalted religious aspirations and genius;
their work transcends time and even all the wide
varieties of religious and philosophical beliefs. For
our purposes, no religious connotations whatsoever
are implied by the use of these biblical divine
names. Anyone may use them without subscribing
in the least to the ancient religious views, whether

he or she be a Jew, Christian, Hindu, Buddhist, Moslem, someone who worships in an indigenous way, an atheist, or anything else.

This is a purely practical, empirical system that is successful regardless of the skepticism or faith of the operator. Today we may consider these sacred names in an entirely different and useful light: They are keynotes of different components of our nature, doorways to so many levels of that part of the psyche that is usually subconscious. They are vibratory rates or symbolic signatures of the psychophysical centers we are describing. Their use as vibratory keynotes awakens into activity the centers with which their rate is in sympathy, and conveys to our consciousness some recognition of the many levels of the subconscious spiritual side of our personalities. The actual religious significance of these names does not concern us, nor do their literal translations.

Let us focus again on the Air center in the throat, and let the vibratory sounds be intoned a number of times, until their existence is recognized and clearly felt as a definite sensory experience. There is no mistaking the sensation of its awakening. About the same length of time should be spent here, and in the following centers, as was devoted to the contemplation of the Spirit center. Once this period of time has elapsed, let it, with the aid of the imagination, thrust a shaft of light downward from itself.

The light descends to the solar plexus region, just beneath the sternum or breastbone, and the shaft expands once again to form a third sphere. This is the position of the Fire center.

The allocation of fire to this center is particularly appropriate, for the heart is usually associated with the emotions, with love and the higher feelings. The diameter of this sphere should extend from the front of the body to the back. The name to vibrate here is *Jehovah Eloah ve-Daas*, pronounced *Yeh-hoh-vah Eh-loh ve-Dah-ahs*. Words to vibrate here are *I love*.

Take care that the intonation vibrates well within the white or golden sphere. If this is done, a radiation of warmth will be felt to emanate from the center, gently stimulating all the parts and organs around it.

Since the mind functions in and through the body, being coextensive with it, the mental and emotional faculties likewise become stimulated by the dynamic flow of energy from the centers. The seemingly solid barrier between our conscious and subconscious minds — an armored partition that impedes our free expression and hinders spiritual development — slowly begins to dissolve. As time goes on, and the practice continues, it may disappear completely and the personality gradually achieves integration and wholeness. Genuine health spreads to every function of mind and body, and happiness follows as a permanent blessing.

Continue the shaft downward from the solar plexus to the pelvic region, the region of the generative organs: the Water center. Visualize here, too, a radiant sphere of approximately the same dimensions as the higher one. Intone here, too, a name that produces a rapid vibration in the cells and molecules of the tissue in that region: *Shaddai El Chai*, pronounced *Shah-di El Chi* (the *ch* is guttural, as in "loch"). The words to intone here are *I create*.

Let the mind dwell on the sphere and the words (or the pure vibration, if you choose) for some minutes, visualizing the sphere as a white or golden brilliance. Each time the mind wanders from such a brilliance, as in the beginning it is bound to do, let it gently be coaxed back by repeated and powerful vibrations of the name or words or tone you associate with the center.

It may be feared that this practice will awaken or stimulate sexual feelings and emotions unnecessarily. For those who are feeling sexual conflicts, for any of a number of reasons, such an apprehension may be legitimate.

Actually, however, the fear is groundless: The contemplation of the Water center as a sphere of white or golden light connected by a shaft to the higher centers acts more as a sedative than as a stimulant. And, in point of fact, sexual stimulation can be very effectively dealt with — not by repression, but by the circulation of such energies through the system by means of this practice. A thoroughgoing and far-reaching process of sublimation, almost truly alchemical in effect, may be achieved. (This is not, however, to be construed as encouraging the avoidance of dealing effectively with sexual problems, through whatever form of therapy is necessary.)

The final step is to visualize the shaft descending once more from the reproductive sphere, moving downward through the thighs and legs until it strikes the feet. There it expands and forms a fifth sphere. We have named this one the Earth center.

Let the mind visualize here exactly as before a brilliant, dazzling sphere of the same size as the others. Vibrate the name *Adonai ha-Aretz,* pronounced *Ah-doh-ni hah-Ah-retz,* or use the words *I bless.*

Spend several minutes awakening this center by fixed and steady thought and by repeated intonation, then pause for a short while.

Try to clearly visualize the entire shaft of silvery or golden light, studded as it were with five gorgeous diamonds of incomparable brilliance, stretching from the crown of the head to the soles of the feet. A few minutes is usually enough time to give reality to this concept, and bring about a vivid realization of the powerful forces that, playing upon the personality, are eventually assimilated into the physical, mental, and emotional system after their transformation and passage through the imaginative centers.

The combination of rhythmic breathing with the willed visualization of the descent of power through the light shaft or Middle Pillar, as it is also called, produces by far the best results.

Adding Color

As skill and familiarity are acquired in the for-mulation of the centers, an addition to the tech-nique may be made. Earlier I remarked that color was an important consideration in this technique. Each center has a different color attribution, though it is wisest for a long period of time to refrain from using any other color than white or gold.

To the Spirit or coronal center, the color white or gold is attributed. It is the color of purity, spirit, divinity, and so on. It represents, not so much a human element, but a universal and cosmic princi-ple overshadowing the whole of humankind. As we descend the shaft, however, the colors change.

Lavender is attributed to the Air or throat center, and it represents particularly the mental faculties, human consciousness as such.

To the Fire center, red is an obvious associa-tion.

Blue is the color ascribed to the Water center; it is the color of peace, calmness, and tranquility, concealing enormous strength and virility. In other words, its peace is the peace of strength and power rather than the inertia of weakness.

Finally, the color ascribed to the lowest center of Earth is russet, the rich, deep color of the earth itself, the foundation upon which we rest.

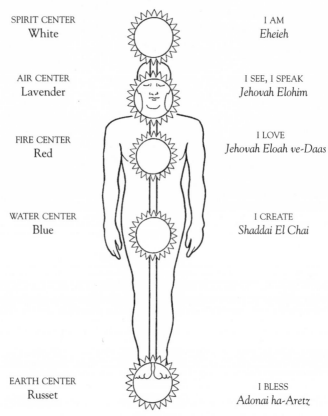

SPIRIT CENTER
White

I AM
Eheieh

AIR CENTER
Lavender

I SEE, I SPEAK
Jehovah Elohim

FIRE CENTER
Red

I LOVE
Jehovah Eloah ve-Daas

WATER CENTER
Blue

I CREATE
Shaddai El Chai

EARTH CENTER
Russet

I BLESS
Adonai ha-Aretz

From this brief and concise summary, it can be seen that each of these centers has an affinity or sympathy with a different spiritual component. One center is sympathetic to or associated with the emotions and feelings, while another has a definite intellectual quality. It follows logically, therefore — and experience demonstrates this fact — that stimulating these centers and gradually bringing them into a state of balance and equilibrium evokes a sympathetic reaction from every part of our nature.

Where disease is manifesting in the body, the activity of the appropriate center must be considered as affected somehow in an unhealthy way. Its stimulation by thought, sound, and color tends to stimulate the corresponding psychic principle and thus disperses the maladjustment. Sooner or later a reaction is induced physically in the disappearance of the disease, and the consequent building up of new cells and tissues: the manifestation of health itself.

3

The Art of True Healing

Although I have stressed the healing of physical ills, it cannot be insisted upon too strongly that this method is suitable for application to a host of other problems, whether it be a problem of poverty, character development, social or marital difficulties — in fact any type of problem one has.

Now we're ready for another very important stage in the development of the Middle Pillar technique: circulating energy.

Circulating the Force

Having brought power and spiritual energy into the system by means of visualizing the centers, how best are we to use it? That is to say, use it in such a way that every single cell, every atom, every organ becomes stimulated and vitalized by that dynamic stream?

To begin, we throw the mind upward to the coronal sphere again, and imagine it to be in a state of vigorous activity. It revolves rapidly, absorbing spiritual energy from space around it, and transforming it in such a way that it becomes available for immediate use in any human activity.

Imagine, then, that this transformed energy flows like a stream down the left side of the head, down the left side of the trunk and the left leg. While the current is descending, the breath should slowly be exhaled to a convenient rhythm. Then slowly inhale, and imagine that the vital current passes from the sole of the left foot to the right foot, and gradually ascends the right side of the body. In this way it returns to the source from which it was issued — the coronal center, the human source of all energy and vitality — establishing a closed electrical circuit.

Visualize this energy flowing within the body rather than traveling around the periphery of the physical body. It is an interior psychic circulation rather than a purely physical one. Once this circulation is firmly established by the mind, let it flow evenly to the rhythm of your breathing for some seconds so that the circuit has been traversed about half a dozen times — or even more, if you wish.

Then repeat it in a slightly different direction. Visualize the vital flow as moving from the coronal center above the head down the back of the head and body. It turns forward under the soles of the feet and ascends up the front of the body in a fairly wide belt of vibrating energy. This should also be accompanied by a slow, steady exhalation and inhalation of breath, and should continue for at least six complete circuits.

The general effect of these two movements is to establish in and about the physical form an ovoid shape (shaped somewhat like an egg) of swiftly circulating substance and power. Since the spiritual energy dealt with by this technique is extremely dynamic and kinetic, it radiates in every direction, spreading outward to an appreciable distance.

It is this radiation that forms, colors, and informs the ovoid sphere of sensation, which is not limited to the shape or dimension of the physical frame. General perception and experience has it that the sphere of luminosity and magnetism extends outward to a distance more or less identical to the length of the outstretched arm. And it is within this aura, as we may call it, that the physical person exists rather like a kernel within a nutshell.

Circulating the force admitted into the system by these mental exercises is tantamount to charging it to a considerable degree in every aspect of its nature with life and energy. Naturally this is bound to exert a considerable influence, so far as general health is concerned, upon the enclosed "kernel" within.

The final method of circulation resembles the action of a fountain. Just as water is forced or drawn up through a pipe until it jets up above, and falls in a spray on all sides, so does the power directed by this last circulation.

Now throw the mind downward to the Earth center, and imagine it to be the culmination of all the others, the receptacle of all power, the storehouse and terminal of the incoming vital force.

Then imagine that this power ascends, or is drawn or sucked upward by the magnetic attraction of the Spirit center above the crown of the head. The power ascends the shaft until it surges overhead with a marvelous fountainous display and falls down within the confines of the ovoid aura.

When it has descended to the feet, it is again gathered together and concentrated in the Earth center before it surges up the shaft again.

The fountain circulation should accompany a definite rhythm of inhalation and exhalation. By these means, the healing force is distributed to every part of the body. No single atom or cell in any organ or limb is omitted from the influence of its healing, regenerative power.

The Art of True Healing

Once the circulations are completed, let the mind dwell quietly on the idea of the

sphere of light, spiritual and vital and healing, surrounding the entire body. The visualization should be made as vivid and as
powerful as possible.

The sensation following the partial or
complete formulation of the aura in the
manner described is so marked and definite
as to be quite unmistakable. It is marked by
an extreme sense of calmness and vitality
and poise, as though the mind was placid
and still. The body, completely at rest, feels
in all its parts thoroughly charged and permeated by the vibrant current of life.
The skin over all the body feels a gentle
prickling and warmth, caused by the inten-
sification of life within. The eyes become
clear and bright, the skin takes on a fresh,
healthy glow, and every faculty — spiritual,
mental, emotional, and physical — becomes considerably enhanced.

If there are any functional disturbances
in any organ or limb, this is the moment
when the attention should be directed and
focused on that part. The result of this focus

of attention directs a flow of energy over and above the general equilibrium just established. The diseased organ becomes bathed in a sea of light and power. Diseased tissue and diseased cells, under the stimulus of such power, become gradually broken down and ejected from the personal sphere. The revitalized bloodstream is then able to send to that spot new nourishment and new life so that new cells, tissue, fiber, etc., can easily be built up. In this way, health is restored by the persistent concentration of divine power.

When this is carried on for a few days in the case of superficial ailments, and for months in the event of chronic and severe troubles, all symptoms may successfully be banished without others coming to take their place. There is no suppression of symptoms; the result of these methods is elimination of the disease.

Even mental and emotional problems may be effectively dealt with by using these techniques, for the currents of force arise from the deepest strata of the subconscious mind, where mental and emotional neuroses have their origin — where they lock up our natural energy, preventing spontaneous and free expression of the psyche. The upwelling of vital forces through the entire system dissolves the crystallizations and armored barriers that divide the various strata of psychic function.

Where physical disease is the problem to be attacked, the procedure to follow is slightly different — and, if the problem is serious, one should still of course consult a competent physician. In this instance a considerably stronger current of force is necessary in order to dissolve any abnormalities, such as growths or lesions, and to set in motion the systemic and metabolic activities to construct new tissue and cellular structure.

To fulfill these conditions, it is ideally very helpful to have a second person to assist, so that his or her vitality may be added to that of the sufferer in order to overcome the condition. Here is a useful technique — one that my experience has discovered to be supremely successful, and one that anyone can adopt:

First of all, completely relax every tissue in the body before attempting the Middle Pillar technique. The patient is placed in a highly relaxed state by first simply becoming aware of every neuromuscular tension. Consciousness is then able to eliminate tension and induce a relaxed state of that muscle or limb.

Spinal manipulation and massage, with deep kneading, is very useful to begin with, for in this way an enhanced circulation of the blood and lymph system is produced — and, from the physiological point of view, half the battle is won.

Once a suitable degree of relaxation is obtained, the patient's feet are crossed over the ankles and the patient's fingers interlaced so that they rest lightly over the solar plexus. The operator or healer then sits on the right side of the person if the patient is right-handed (and on the left for a

left-handed patient) and places his or her
right hand gently on the solar plexus under
the patient's intertwined hands, and his or
her left hand on the patient's head (these
are reversed for a left-handed patient). A
form of rapport is established at once, and
within a few minutes a free circulation of
magnetism and vitality is set up, easily dis-
cernable by both patient and healer.

The patient's attitude should be one of
absolute receptivity to the incoming force
— this will naturally occur if the patient
has unwavering confidence and faith in the
operator's integrity and ability. Silence and
quiet should be maintained for a short
while; then the operator silently focuses on
his or her own body and performs the practice of the Middle Pillar, still maintaining
physical contact with the patient.

The healer's awakened spiritual centers
act on the patient by sympathy. A similar
awakening is introduced within the patient's
sphere, whose centers eventually begin to
operate and throw a stream of energy into

his or her system. Even when the operator
does not vibrate the divine names audibly,
the power flowing through his or her fingers
sets up an energy that produces healing
activity within the patient, whose psycho-
spiritual centers are sympathetically stirred
into the active assimilation and projection
of force so that, without any conscious effort
on the patient's part, his or her sphere is
infused with, even invaded by, the divine
power of healing and life.

When the operator arrives at the circulation stage, the operator employs his or her
visualizing faculty — a veritable magical
power indeed — so that the augmented
currents of energy flow not only through his
or her own sphere but through that of the
patient as well.

The nature of their rapport now begins
to undergo a subtle change. Whereas for-
merly there existed close sympathy and a
harmonious frame of mind, mutually held,
during and after the circulations there is an
actual union and interblending of the two

energy fields. They unite to form a single continuous sphere as the interchange and transference of vital energy proceeds. The healer — or the healer's subconscious psyche or spiritual self — is able to divine exactly how strong the projected current should be, and precisely where it should be directed.

A number of treatments incorporating the cooperation and training of the patient in the use of these methods should certainly go far in alleviating the original condition. If necessary, medical and manipulative methods may usefully be combined with the methods described to facilitate and hasten the cure.

Although I have stressed healing of physical ills, it cannot be insisted upon too strongly that this method is suitable for application to a host of other problems. This technique will be found to be a powerful creative tool in all other situations that may arise, whether it be a problem of poverty, character development, social or marital difficulties — in fact, any type of problem one has.

4

Tuning Ourselves
to the Infinite

Prayer is indispensable. The wish, the heart's desire, the goal to be reached, must be held firmly in mind, vitalized by divine power, and propelled forward into the universe by the fiery intensity of all the emotional exaltation we are capable of.

Repetition is often invaluable both in teaching and in learning new subjects, so some recapitulation of the various processes involved in the Middle Pillar practice will help to clarify some of the issues. And I would like to add a further consideration that helps to render the entire method more effective, and lifts it to a higher plane of understanding and achievement. This final step enables us to call into operation dynamic factors within us that aid in the production of any desired results.

The first step, as we have seen, is a physical, mental, and emotional exercise that allows us to relax, and to loosen the chronic grip of neuromuscular tensions. Every involuntary tension in any group of muscles or tissues in any area of the body must be brought within the scope of conscious awareness. Awareness is the magical key by which such tension may literally be melted away and dissolved.

Only a little practice is necessary for this, and skill is very quickly and easily obtained. As physical relaxation is achieved, the mind itself in all its different aspects and ramifications undergoes a similar relaxation.

Physical inflexibility as well as mental and emotional tension are the great barriers to realizing the omnipresence of the body of God. They actually prevent one from becoming aware of the everpresence of the life-force, the dependence of the mind upon — and even its ultimate identity with — the Universal Mind, the collective unconscious. When the mind's petty barriers are eliminated, and life flows through its extensive organization, we become conscious of the dynamic principle pervading and permeating all things. This step is without question the all-important phase in the application of these techniques.

Once aware of this, the logical procedure is to

awaken the inner spiritual centers that can handle this high-voltage power, and transform it into a usable human quality. Possibly the easiest way to conceive of this is to liken the spiritual part of us to a radio receiver. A receiver must first of all be connected to a power source before it will work. Once power is flowing through it, then the rest of the intricate mechanism is able to come into operation.

So also with us: We can tune ourselves to the infinite more readily through the mechanism of lighting up our inner centers, our own built-in receiver. When the receiver is operative, the divine current can flow through it in various ways, until both body and mind become powerfully vitalized and strengthened with spiritual energy.

But all this is merely preparatory. The radio may have power flowing through it, and the equipment in perfect operating condition — but what do we want to do with it? So also with us.

Perhaps sickness is present. Or we need money. Or we have undesirable moral or mental traits — or whatnot. We can elevate our minds by utilizing this energy, so that the desire of our heart automatically realizes itself with practically no effort at all.

The wish, the heart's desire, the goal to be reached, must be held firmly in mind, vitalized by divine power, and propelled forward into the universe by the fiery intensity of all the emotional exaltation we are capable of. Prayer is therefore indispensable. Prayer, not merely as a petition to some God outside of us somewhere, but prayer conceived as the spiritual and emotional stimulus calculated to bring about an identification with or realization of our own Godhead.

Prayer, if sincerely undertaken, mobilizes all the qualities of the self, and the inner fervor that it awakens reinforces the work previously done. Prayer renders success an almost infallible result. For in such a case, success comes not because of one's own human effort, but because God brings about the result. The fervor and the emotional exaltation enable one to realize the divinity within, which is the spiritual factor that brings our desires to immediate and complete fulfillment.

An ancient metaphysician once said, *Inflame thyself with prayer.*

Here is the secret. We must pray so that the whole of our being becomes aflame with a spiritual intensity before which nothing can stand. All illusions and all limitations fade away utterly before this fervor. When the soul literally burns up, then spiritual identity with God is attained. Then the heart's desire is accomplished without effort — because God does it. The wish becomes fact — objective, phenomenal fact, for all to see.

What prayers, then, should be employed to lift the mind to this intensity, to awaken the emotional fervor so that one can "inflame thyself in praying"? This is a problem to be solved by each one of us for ourselves. Every one of us has some idea about prayer which, when sustained, will inflame us to inward realization. Some use the words of their own heart. Some use words of their own traditions. Some use a poem that has always had the effect of exalting them. Some use the Lord's Prayer, or the Twenty-third Psalm — and so on for all possible types of people from all different traditions.

5

Other Uses of
the Technique

By stimulating our centers within and then formulating clearly and vividly our demands upon the universe, we are capable of attracting almost anything we require. . . .

As I have suggested before, there are other uses of the Middle Pillar technique, quite apart from therapy. If you practice the technique, and if you are enterprising, you will divine your own uses for it.

It may be for various reasons that certain physical necessities of life, or certain mental, emotional, or spiritual qualities have been denied one — with a subsequent sense of frustration and a limiting effect on character. Frustration always has a depressing and inhibitory effect on the human mind, producing indecision, inefficiency, and a sense of inferiority.

There is no real necessity for any undue frustration and inhibition in our lives. A certain amount is no doubt inevitable. As long as we remain human it is quite certain that in some measure we are likely to be thwarted in our efforts to fully express the inner self, and consequently experience some degree of frustration. But any abnormal measure or persistent sense of frustration or lack of accomplishment may be dealt with and eliminated by these mental, emotional, and spiritual methods.

First of all, an understanding of life is essential, as well as an unconditional acceptance of everything in life and every experience that may come one's way. With understanding comes a love of life and living, for love and understanding are one and the same. Understanding also fosters the determination to no longer frustrate natural processes but, by our acceptance, to cooperate with nature.

A vast number of mental, emotional, and spiritual methods have been developed that have long held out hope that these inhibitory conditions may be alleviated. Poverty of estate as well as of idea is a life condition that these techniques have always proven effective in treating.

One effective method is deep and prolonged

reflection upon just the mental stimulus, moral quality, or material thing that is wanted, so that the idea of the need sinks into the subconscious mind. If the barriers leading to the subconscious are penetrated so that the subconscious accepts the idea of the need, then sooner or later life will inevitably attract those things required.

But, as with all therapeutic methods, there are so many instances where, despite close adherence to the prescribed techniques, success is not forthcoming. It is my feeling and belief that they fail for very much the same reasons that their healing efforts fail: because there is not true understanding of the nature of the subconscious and of the whole body-mind organism whereby such effects can be produced. There is no appreciation of the methods by which the dynamic nature of the subconscious can be stimulated so that the human personality becomes transformed into a powerful magnet attracting to itself whatever it truly desires or is necessary to its welfare.

Some people question whether this procedure is morally defensible. The answer is brief:

Whatever facilities we have are meant to be used, and used both for our own advantage and that of others. If we are in a state of constant mental friction, emotional frustration, and excessive poverty, we can be of little service either to ourselves or others. When we eliminate these restrictions and improve our mental and emotional faculties so that our spiritual nature is able to penetrate through the personality and manifest itself in practical ways, then we are in a position to be of some service to others.

By stimulating our centers of energy within and then formulating clearly and vividly our demands upon the universe, we are capable of attracting almost anything we require — as long, naturally, as it exists within the bounds of reason and possibility.

I wish to introduce here one other very powerful and effective element, one that borrows from astrology. I am not concerned here with astrology as such, merely that it is convenient to use its schema, its system of classification. I am not in the least concerned about arguing for or against the validity of astrology; I simply want to state that, from a practical point of view, the basic components of astrology are of great value in that they offer a concise classification of the broad division of things.*

The roots of astrology are in the seven principal ideas, symbolized by the sun, moon, and inner planets — the planets known to our ancestors. Every idea and thing we can imagine can be classified within one of these root ideas. To each of them there is attributed a positive and negative color, and a divine name for the purpose of vibration.

These things vary somewhat from tradition to tradition; I propose naming the principal attributes as follows:

Sun: Power and success. Life, money, growth of all kinds. Illumination, imagination, mental power. Health. Superiors, employers, executives, officials. Positive color: orange. Negative color: yellow or

---

Editor's Note: Carl Jung and Joseph Campbell would both agree wholeheartedly. Using these symbols is not essential, however, for effective use of the Middle Pillar meditation.

gold. *Jehovah Eloah ve-Daas*, pronounced *Yeh-hoh-vah El-loh ve-Dah-ahs*.

Moon: Changes and fluctuations. Women, intuition. The personality. The general public. Short journeys, moving to a new home or new area. Positive color: blue. Negative color: puce (a dark red). *Shaddai El Chai*, pronounced *Shad-di El Chi* (the *ch* is guttural, as in "loch").

Mercury: Business matters, writing, contracts, judgment, short travels. Buying, selling, bargaining. Neighbors, giving and obtaining information. Literary capabilities, intellectual friends. Books, papers. Positive color: yellow. Negative color: orange. *Elohim Tzavoos*, pronounced *Eh-loh-heem Tsah-voh-ohs*.

Venus: Social affairs, relationships, affections and emotions, women, younger people. All pleasures and the arts, music, beauty, extravagance, luxury, and even self-indulgence. Positive and negative color: emerald green. *Jehovah Tzavoos*, pronounced *Yeh-hoh-vah Tsah-voh-ohs*.

Mars: Energy, willpower, haste, anger, construction or destruction (according to application), danger, surgery. Vitality and magnetism. Positive and negative color: bright red. *Elohim Gibor*, pronounced *Eh-loh-heem Gi-bor*.

Jupiter: Abundance growth, expansion, and generosity. Spirituality, visions, dreams, long journeys. Bankers, creditors, debtors, gambling. Positive color: purple. Negative color: blue. *El*, pronounced exactly as written.

Saturn: Older people and old plans. Debts and their repayment. Agriculture, real estate, death, wills, stability, inertia. Positive color: indigo. Negative color: black. *Jehovah Elohim*, pronounced *Yeh-hoh-vah Eh-loh-heem*.

These very briefly are the attributions of the sun, moon, and planets under which almost everything and every subject in nature may be classified. This classification is extremely useful because it enormously simplifies one's task of physical and spiritual development. I'll give a few simple examples to illustrate the function and method of employing these correspondences.

Suppose I am engaged in certain studies requiring books that are not easily obtainable from booksellers. Despite my every demand for them, in spite of widespread advertising and willingness to pay a reasonable price for them, my efforts are unavailing. The result is that, for the time being, my studies are held up. The delay becomes excessive and irritating, and I decide to use my own technical methods for ending it.

At certain prescribed intervals, preferably upon awakening in the morning and before retiring to sleep at night, I practice the rhythmic breathing and the Middle Pillar. By these methods I have made available enormous quantities of spiritual power, and transformed the subconscious into a powerful storage battery, ready to project or attract power to fulfill my need. This I circulate through the auric system.

My next step consists of visualizing the negative or passive color of Mercury — orange — so that meditating upon it changes the surrounding auric color to that hue. Orange is used because books, which I need, are attributed to Mercury, and I employ the negative color because it tends to make the sphere of sensation open, passive, and receptive.

Then I proceed to charge and vitalize the sphere by vibrating the appropriate divine name again and again, until it seems to my perceptions that all the mercurial forces of the universe react to the magnetic attraction of that sphere. All the forces of the universe are imagined to converge upon my sphere, attracting to me just those books, documents, critics, friends, and so on, needed to further my work.

Inevitably, after persistent and concentrated work, I hear from friends or booksellers quite by chance, so it seems, that these books are available. Introductions are procured to the right people, and my work is assisted.

The results occur in a perfectly natural way — one is not to imagine that the use of these methods contravenes the known laws of nature and that miraculous phenomena will occur. Far from it; there is nothing in them that is supernatural. These methods are based upon the use of psychic principles normally latent within us, which everyone possesses. No individual is unique in this respect. And the use of these psychic principles brings results through quite normal but unsuspected channels.

Here is another example:

If I desire to help a patient or friend who has literary aspirations but at a certain juncture finds his style cramped and the free flow of ideas inhibited, I should alter my method in one particular point only. Instead of using orange as before, I should visualize the aura as having a yellow or golden color, though the vibratory name would be the same.

Instead of imagining universal forces to have a centripetal motion toward my sphere, I should attempt to realize that the mercurial forces awakened within me by the color visualization and vibration are being projected from me to my patient or friend.

If he, too, becomes quiet and meditative at the same hour, my help becomes more powerful, since he consciously assists my efforts with a similar meditation. But this need not be insisted upon. For, as shown by telepathy experiments, his own unconscious psyche will pick up automatically the inspiration and power I have telepathically forwarded to him *in absentia*. The technique is very effective when the person receiving the energy is asleep, as well.

This system combines telepathic suggestion with the willed communication of vital power. The technical procedure is, as I have shown, extremely simple — even where employed for subjective ends.

Suppose the realization suddenly comes to me that instead of being the magnanimous person I had imagined myself to be, I am in fact mean and stingy. Of course I could go to a psychoanalyst to discover why my nature early in life had become warped so that I developed a habit of miserliness. But this is a lengthy and costly business (an especially important consideration for a miser), and so much would depend upon the analyst I chose, and the relationship we would eventually create.

Instead, I might use the following technique.

My first steps consist of those described before: rhythmic breathing, the light-shaft formulated from head to foot, and the circulation of force through the aura. Then, remembering that a generous outlook upon life is a Jupiterian quality, I surround myself with an azure blue sphere while vibrating frequently and powerfully the divine name *El*.

It depends entirely upon one's skill and familiarity with the system whether the names are vibrated silently or audibly. But by either way, powerful Jupiterian currents permeate my being. I even visualize every cell being bathed in an ocean of blue, and I attempt to imagine currents invading my sphere from every direction, so that all my thinking and feeling is literally in terms of blue.

Slowly a subtle transformation ensues — as long as I am really sincere, desirous of correcting my faults, and if I attempt to become generous enough to perform the practice faithfully and often.

Similarly, if a friend or patient complained of a similar vice in him or her, appealing to me for help, in this instance I would use a positive color for projection. I would formulate my sphere as an active, dynamic purple sphere, rich and royal in color, and project its generous, healing, and productive influence upon their mind and personality. Over time, the fault would be corrected to their satisfaction, and their spiritual nature would be enhanced.

And so on, with everything else. These few examples, I am sure, will have shown the application of the methods.

It is not enough simply to wish for certain results and idly expect them to follow. Failure can only come from such an idle course. Anything worthwhile and likely to succeed requires a great deal of work and perseverance. The Middle Pillar technique is certainly no exception. But devotion to it is extremely worthwhile because of the nature and quality of the results that follow.

Once a day will demonstrate the effectiveness of the method. Twice a day is much better — especially if there is some illness or mental or emotional difficulty to overcome.

Those who are sincere and those whose spiritual natures are gradually unfolding will apply themselves to the method quite apart from the promises which I have here held out, simply because it is so enjoyable and fulfilling in itself to do the Middle Pillar meditation.

Healing powers, freedom from poverty and

worry, happiness — all of these are eminently de-sirable. But above all of these is the desirability of knowing and expressing our spiritual nature within — though it may be in some cases that this ideal is hardly attainable until some measure of fulfillment in other respects and on other levels has been achieved.

When, however, the ideal is realized as desir-able, then the value of this method will also be realized as supremely effective to that end.

Afterword
by Marc Allen

If you practice the meditations in this book, I'm sure variations will naturally occur for you. Here are a few variations I've developed over the years that might offer some new possibilities for you.

Afterward, I'll close with a few reflections on the meaning of the Middle Pillar.

The Chakra Meditation

As most of you are probably aware, the five centers Dr. Regardie has us envision in the Middle Pillar meditation closely correspond to the seven chakras of the meditative tradition that originated in India, and is now well-known in the West.

The Spirit center is the *Crown Chakra*, the seventh chakra, our union with the quantum field, with all of creation.

The Air center combines the fifth and sixth chakras, the *Throat Chakra* and the *Third Eye Chakra*. The Throat Chakra is associated with creative expression and, even more broadly, all personal expression. It is in the throat that we give voice to what is in our hearts and minds. The Third Eye Chakra, centered between our eyebrows, is the place of inner vision — the center of our magical power, the center from which we create in our minds those things we desire, and launch into the universe, into the quantum field (and, as Deepak Chopra puts it, "let the universe work out the details").

The Fire center combines the third and fourth chakras, the *Power Center* and the *Heart Chakra*. The Power Center is our major source of physical strength, the center of action in the world (the Japanese call it the *hara*). The Heart Chakra is the central chakra (there are three above, three below). It is the source of love, acceptance, joy. It is our connection to humanity, all the world, and is central to our purpose in life.

The Water center combines the first and

second chakras, the *Root Chakra* and the *Sexual Center*. The Root Chakra is our grounding in the earth, our connection with our source. The Sexual Center is the source of our ability to create life, the true source of all creativity and fulfillment.

The Earth center is below all chakras, at our feet, connecting us to the earth. This serves the same function as the Root Chakra.

Sometimes, in the Middle Pillar meditation, I find it even more effective to focus on each of the seven chakras rather than the five centers of the original tradition. Rather than starting at the top, as in the original meditation, I usually start at the bottom and work up. Experiment with both, and see which you prefer. Here's an example of one form of the chakra meditation:

Sit comfortably, feet on the floor, hands relaxed on your legs, palms up — or (my favorite) lie flat on your back, arms at your sides, palms up. Close your eyes.

If you are lying on your back, you can extend your right arm above your head, if you wish, with palm open, and you can turn your left hand over, so your palm touches the ground. In doing this, you are mirroring the position of the Magician in the tarot cards, the position of manifestation.

Take a deep, relaxing, and cleansing breath. As you exhale, *relax your body*. Take another deep, relaxing breath. As you exhale, *relax your mind*. Take another deep, relaxing breath. As you exhale, *let everything go*.

Count down slowly, from ten to one, imagining you are like a leaf falling from a tree, falling deeper and deeper into quiet relaxation and stillness.

Repeat this process as many times as necessary, until you are in a deeply relaxed, comfortable space.

Focus your attention on your Root Chakra. If you are sitting, you're sitting right on your Root Chakra. If you are lying on your back, it's at the base of your torso, centered in your sphincter muscle and including the muscles around it that are solidly on the ground (your *gluteus maximus*, the largest muscle in your body). Breathe deeply into that area, imagining a warm, healing light filling the area. Some people choose to imagine a flower blooming there — and at each of the other centers as well — often an unfolding, spreading lotus blossom. Let your visualization evolve naturally. A glowing circle or sphere of light will do nicely.

After several breaths, move the sphere of light up to your Sexual Chakra. Breathe deeply into that area, imagining a warm, healing light filling the area.

After several breaths, move the sphere of light up to your Power Center, centered around your navel. Breathe deeply into that area, imagining a warm, healing light filling the area.

After several deep, healing breaths, move the sphere of light up to your heart. Breathe deeply into your heart and chest, imagining a warm, healing light filling the area.

After a few more deep, healing breaths, move the sphere of light up to your throat. Breathe deeply, imagining a warm, healing light filling the area.

After several breaths, move the sphere of light up to your third eye, centered directly between your eyebrows. Breathe deeply, imagining being filled with and surrounded with warm, healing light.

After several breaths, move the sphere to the crown of your head, the top of your skull, the Crown Chakra. Breathe deeply,, and imagine a warm, healing light. Some people imagine a vast unfolding flower here — a lotus with a thousand petals.

Now imagine the light and energy from your Crown Chakra flowing down the right side of your body, as you exhale, and up the left, as you inhale. Do this several times, "running energy" around the Middle Pillar of your body.

Now imagine the light and energy coming from your feet up through the Root

Chakra and up the front of your body, as you inhale, and down the back of your body, as you exhale. Do this several times.

Now imagine the light and energy coming from your feet up through the Root Chakra and right up through the center of your body, traveling through the shining light-filled Middle Pillar of your body, up through your Crown Chakra as you inhale, and showering over your whole body as you exhale, creating a fountain of light and energy and power. As Dr. Regardie describes so beautifully, *it surges overhead with a marvelous fountainous display.*

You are now ready to focus on a specific healing or a specific thing you wish to create in your life. If you wish to heal yourself, bring the focus of your consciousness to whatever part of your body needs healing, and fill it with several light-filled, healing breaths, imagining all sickness dissolving, imagining yourself filled with radiant health.

If you wish to heal someone else, bring

the focus of your consciousness to your third eye, your inner vision. Fill the area with deep, healing breaths, then imagine you are sending healing energy to the person needing healing. This works whether the person is next to you, or distant.

If you wish to create something — anything — in your life, bring the focus of your consciousness to your third eye. Fill the area with several deep breaths, then imagine as clearly as you possibly can with your inner vision what you wish to create in your life. Imagine it as fully formed, completely realized.

Spend some time enjoying your visualization, so you feel *emotionally* exactly how it feels to do, be, and have what you want in your life. If what you want is in alignment with your spiritual being, if you have a clear idea of what you want to create, and if you envision it clearly enough and regularly enough so that you can feel doing, being, or having it, it will soon manifest for you in physical reality.

So be it. So it is.

End your meditation with whatever feels comfortable and appropriate for you: You can let your visualization float off into space, and "let the universe take care of the details"; you can say a prayer; you can imagine the whole planet bathed in the healing light of your radiant meditation; you can meditate quietly, bathed in the light of your inner radiance, watching whatever thoughts arise; you can ask for guidance in your life, and listen for answers from your deepest sources of knowledge; or you can simply sit in wonderful, healing silence.

Finish with a final deep breath, open your eyes, and come back into waking reality, feeling relaxed, refreshed, peaceful, in harmony with yourself and your world.

So be it. So it is.

The above meditation can take anywhere from fifteen minutes to an hour or longer. Using it, I imagined my company's success; I imagined the light-filled home I am sitting in at this moment; I imagined this book, fully realized, and every book

I have ever written or edited, far before each occurred in reality.

I've developed a much shorter version, over the years, when I haven't had that much time. But I encourage everyone to do the above meditation, and spend at least fifteen or twenty minutes on it. It is especially effective just as you awake in the morning (my favorite time to do it), or when you go to bed at night. It's certainly worth getting up fifteen minutes earlier in the morning, if necessary — you can visualize sailing effortlessly through the day, creating success after success (or whatever else you want to create that day).

Especially at first, you'll find your attention will wander. Simply bring it back to where you were, and continue. After a while, your powers of concentration will become stronger, and the feelings and visualizations will become more vivid. It is important, as you progress, to do the meditation in a place where you won't be disturbed. Silence is golden.

The Two-Minute Version

Here is an example of how to abbreviate the

previous meditation so that it can still be effective in a very short time. It takes only seven breaths to get into it; then you focus on the healing or whatever else you want to create, let it go, and get on with your life.

Sit or lie comfortably, as above. Close your eyes.

Take a deep breath, and *relax your body*. Take another deep breath, and *relax your mind*.

Take another deep breath, and *let everything go*.

Take another deep breath, and count down from ten to one, falling, like a leaf from a tree, deeper and deeper into stillness.

Take another deep, cleansing breath, and "run the energy" up one side of your body as you inhale, and down the other side of your body as you exhale.

Take another deep breath, and run the energy up the front of your body as you inhale, and down the back of your body as you exhale.

Take another deep breath, and run the light and energy up the middle of your body, up your spine, your Middle Pillar, as you inhale, then let it shower over you, surrounding you fully, as you exhale.

Repeat the seven breaths above, if necessary, until you are relaxed and quiet.

Now focus on the area to be healed, if you wish, and send cleansing light and breath into the area. Or, if you wish to visualize something, focus on your third eye, fill it with light and breath, and imagine what you want to create. Then let it go and let the universe work out the details.

You can end there or, if you wish, finish with a prayer or a silent meditation, or anything else mentioned at the end of the previous meditation — or anything else you wish. . . .

Take a final, healing breath, open your eyes, and come back into waking reality, feeling relaxed, refreshed, fully awake, calm, clear, peaceful, and fulfilled.

So be it. So it is.

A Simple Variation

Relax, as above.

Pick one of the five centers, or one of the seven chakras, and focus your attention on it. Breathe into it, repeatedly, in silence.

Explore its meaning for you, and discover the healing that occurs within it when you quietly meditate upon it.

Personal and Business Relationships

Here is a fascinating variation that has proven to be surprisingly effective in personal relationships. If you are having difficulty with someone in any way — whether in personal life or in business relationships — this meditation can have powerful results.

After you do some form of the Middle Pillar meditation — relaxing, visualizing your energy centers, running energy —

breathe deeply into your heart, and fill it with light. Then imagine the person you are having difficulty with and, from your heart, speak your truth to them. Tell them every-thing you want them to hear. Try not to blame them or make them wrong. Stay in your heart, if at all possible. Try to come from a place of love. Then let the problem go, and meditate on acceptance of the situation.

End with the serenity prayer, or some adaptation of it, if it seems appropriate for you: *God grant me the serenity to accept the things I cannot change, the courage to change the things I can, and the wisdom to know the difference.*

The next time you talk to that person, you will probably be surprised at the change in your rela-tionship. I've seen, many times over many years, seemingly intractable problems between people simply dissolve, and a wonderful warmth emerge between them. You discover, underneath it all, you're really very fond of that person — otherwise, you wouldn't have bothered to be so upset.

This form of creative meditation seems to work even better when the other person is asleep. If you're ever bothered in the middle of the night by a problem with someone, I highly recommend this meditation. And prepare yourself for some truly startling results.

If you try to remain in your heart center in all of your relationships, so many problems simply dissolve, without effort, struggle, or argument. This meditation reminds us of that.

Reflections on the Middle Pillar

Why is it called the Middle Pillar meditation? I think Dr. Regardie assumed the readers of *The Art of True Healing* would be familiar with most of his other books, and at least some of the other books that were popular at the time he was writing — now over sixty years ago. Much of the following material comes from *The Tree of Life* and other books by Israel Regardie.

The Middle Pillar is the main "trunk" of the Tree of Life, the central focus of the study of the

Kabalah, which — along with an Egyptian influence — forms the basis for so much of the Western tradition of metaphysics and magical creation. The Tree of Life has ten stages — beginning in the highest spiritual planes and descending into planes of thought, then emotion, and finally physical reality. *The roots of the Tree of Life are in heaven.* This is a well-known phrase to those who have studied Kabalah. When we understand the Tree of Life, we understand the nature and mechanics of creation, and we become magicians in the true sense of the word, able to magically create what we want in life with the magical power of our understanding.

The four stages that form the Middle Pillar of the Tree of Life are the four stages that every created thing has passed through: First it was (and still in essence is) a spiritual impulse, a form of energy, ever mysterious, connected inexorably on a quantum level with the whole universe.

Then, it becomes a *thought*. Nothing is ever created without first being a thought, a clear thought in the mind. If that thought is held onto long enough, if it is focused upon strongly, it has a chance of manifesting — if, and only if, the thought becomes an *emotion*. In order to create anything, it must not only be envisioned, it must be *desired emotionally*. It must be a feeling within you as well as a thought. This is my interpretation of what Dr. Regardie means when he tells us to "inflame ourselves with prayer." We must strongly feel that we want to create whatever it is we desire in our lives.

Once these three things are in alignment, the Middle Pillar is nearly complete: We have a spiritual impulse that becomes a thought, and that thought becomes a powerful feeling. Once we continue to hold that thought and feeling, so that both our thoughts and feelings become focused instead of scattered, the final stage of the Middle Pillar comes into being, and we create that which we desire, seemingly by magic, in physical reality.

So be it. So it is.

I'll close with a brief meditation on the Kabalah. It will give you a visual picture of the stages of the Tree of Life. Note that the Middle Pillar runs down the center, and that the top circle represents the spiritual stage, the Spirit center; the one directly underneath it represents the stage of thought, the Air center; the one directly underneath that is the stage of emotion, the Water center; and the final stage, at the bottom, is the physical plane, the Earth center. It is here that our desires finally manifest. The roots of creation, the roots of the Tree of Life, are in heaven; its final flowering is in physical reality, in the things we see, hear, smell, taste, and touch.

In the beginning was the endless void, symbolized by the number zero, pure shining infinity, absolute oneness....

○

Then the essence of the miracle of creation occurs, first on the subtlest spiritual and quantum levels of existence, the most wondrous thing in the universe: The one becomes the Two.... The second and third stages of the Tree of Life, the Father and the Mother, appear.

○

○   ○

The Spiritual Plane

All this takes place on the highest spiritual levels, in subtle forms, beyond all words of description. Within it — and this is as mysterious as its source, as mysterious as the energy of a subatomic particle — is an urge for creation.

This creative urge is reflected to a denser level, the level of thought.... Creation becomes a thought...and there are six stages:

The Spiritual Plane

The Mental Plane

Then, if the thought continues — if it is focused upon, and repeated, and not simply let go — it is reflected to a still denser level, the emotional level. Creation becomes a feeling, a desire.... And there are nine stages to the Tree of Life:

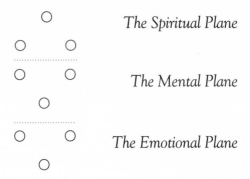

Then, once the Middle Pillar of the spiritual, mental, and emotional planes is in alignment — once our impulse for creation of anything in our life is not only a spiritual impulse but a focused thought and a strong emotion as well — the material plane becomes manifest, in all its splendor: the physical plane, which we can see, touch, feel. The tenth and final stage of the Tree of Life comes into being:

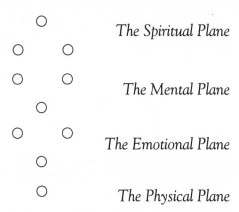

The Spiritual Plane

The Mental Plane

The Emotional Plane

The Physical Plane

The Tree of Life is a map of the process of creation — if we understand that map.

Another thing is certainly worth taking note of: There is one symbol that connects and unifies the entire journey of creation, the whole Tree of Life; one symbol that encompasses all of the forces of creation, the power of God.... It is the key to the mystery of life, and the source of the magical power that we have within us to create and to heal:

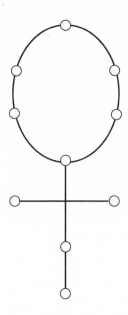

It is Venus: the symbol for woman, the symbol of the power of love, centered in the heart.

The end of all wisdom is love, love, love.
— Sai Baba

A new law I give unto you: Love one another, as I have loved you.
— Jesus

Amen.

Dr. F. I. Regardie has been hailed as one of the most important figures of twentieth-century healing and mysticism. He was born in London in 1907, and first traveled to the United States in 1920. He wrote seventeen books between 1932 and 1972; his most voluminous work, *The Golden Dawn*, is a monumental study of Western magical ritual. *The Art of True Healing* is considered to be his most brilliant and concise work on the powerful effects of focused meditation.

He was a therapist and chiropractor as well as a writer, practicing a form of psychotherapy based on the work of Dr. Wilhelm Reich.

Recommended Reading

If you found value and meaning in *The Art of True Healing*, we recommend the following books and audio cassettes from New World Library:

The Seven Spiritual Laws of Success by Deepak Chopra. A practical guide to the fulfillment of your dreams. An international bestseller, and for a very good reason. Available on audio as well.

Creative Visualization by Shakti Gawain. The classic work (in print for 20 years, three million copies sold) that shows us how to use the power of our imagination to create what we want in life. Available on audio as well, in two formats: the complete book on tape, and selected meditations from the book.

As You Think by James Allen. This classic has inspired readers for nearly a century. The key to our happiness and personal power is in our minds, and this book gives us the key that unlocks the door to our success, however we choose to define that success.

Visionary Business — An Entrepreneur's Guide to Success by Marc Allen. This book can teach you to become a visionary, and create success in business and in life in general — however you define it. Available on audio as well.

Simple Truths by Kent Nerburn. Clear and gentle guidance on the big issues in life. Elegant, profound, and inspiring.

The Wonders of Solitude, edited by Dale Salwak. A deeply moving, inspiring reminder, in the form of three hundred quotations from the world's great writers, of the importance and power of solitude.

New World Library publishes books and
other forms of communication
on the leading edge of personal and
planetary evolution.

For a catalog of our complete library
of fine books and cassettes, contact:

New World Library
14 Pamaron Way
Novato, CA 94949

Phone: (415) 884-2100
Fax: (415) 884-2199
Or call toll-free: (800) 972-6657